The Mea Millennium

Revelation 20 and Millennial Expectation

Michael Gilbertson

Assistant Curate, St Matthew's, Surbiton

GROVE BOOKS LIMITED
RIDLEY HALL RD CAMBRIDGE CB3 9HU

Contents

1. Approaching the Millennium 3

2. Reading the Book of Revelation 6

3. Four Interpretations of the Text 9

4. The Origin of the Symbol of the Millennium 14

5. Making the Millennium Relevant 16

6. Conclusion 23

Bibliography 24

The Cover Illustration is by Peter Ashton

First Impression September 1997
ISSN 1365-490X
ISBN 1 85174 354 5

1
Approaching the Millennium

'Watching, waiting, and working for the millennium...has become, even more than baseball, America's favourite pastime.'[1] This remark, made in 1979, is as true now as it was then. Millennial expectation is a striking characteristic of the church today, and not just in North America. It is especially marked in the fast-growing churches outside the industrialized West, for example in South America and East Asia. Expectation of the end times shows itself in many ways. At one extreme, fears of nuclear holocaust merge with predictions of Armageddon. At the other, magazines carry advertisements for the $50 Quartz Rapture Watch, marked 'One Hour Nearer the Lord's Return.'

In the late twentieth century, expectations of the arrival of the millennium of Revelation 20 have, inevitably, often become entwined with anticipation of the year 2000. As such, this needs to be seen against a wider background of end-time expectation, which goes far beyond the Christian churches. Expectation of radical change associated with the coming turn of the calendrical millennium is characteristic of much New Age thinking. Certain fringe groups which have recently come to attention for tragic reasons such as the Branch Davidians in Waco and the Aum Shinrikyo cult in Japan have been driven by a powerful conviction that the end is near.

In this booklet, I am not attempting a general survey of contemporary eschatology in all its forms.[2] Neither am I dealing specifically with the approach of the year 2000.[3] Instead, I am focusing on one element of biblical eschatology, the millennium, or thousand-year kingdom, which appears in Revelation 20.1–6. This passage stands near the end of the great central section of Revelation, which runs from chapter 4 through to chapter 20, tracing the establishment of divine sovereignty on earth, and the vindication of the people of God. It follows the vision of the rider on the white horse (19.11–21), usually taken to represent the *parousia*, the second coming of Christ. Chapter 20 opens with the descent of an angel from heaven (20.1). He seizes Satan, and binds him in the bottomless pit for a thousand years (20.2). Those who have been killed for their faith in Christ come to life and reign with him for a thousand years (20.4–6). At the end of the thousand years, Satan is

---

1 Leonard Sweet, 'Millennialism in America: Recent Studies,' *Theological Studies* 40 (September 1979) p 531.
2 For a comprehensive recent survey, see Damian Thompson, *The End of Time: Faith and Fear in the Shadow of the Millennium* (London: Sinclair-Stevenson, 1996).
3 *Celebrating the Millennium in the Local Church*, by Michael Rees, published earlier this year in the Grove Evangelism Series, offers excellent practical suggestions for local church activities linked to the year 2000.

released from the pit and leads a final rebellion, which ends with his being cast into the lake of fire (20.10). The scene of the last judgment (20.11–15) is then followed by the descent of the New Jerusalem from heaven (21.1ff).

For various reasons, the millennium is a passage about which many in the major Christian denominations in Britain feel uneasy, and it rarely finds its way into sermons or Bible studies. The aim of this booklet is to try to show that the millennium is in fact a symbol of great theological depth on which the church would do well to reflect more seriously.

On one level, it would be easy to ridicule the more crass excesses of the eschatology industry, such as the Rapture Watch, or 'Beam Me Up, Lord' bumper stickers. But under the surface lie deeply-felt and legitimate concerns. Expectation of imminent tribulation, to be followed by the radical execution of divine justice on the earth, offers a framework within which to locate contemporary fears and insecurities about law and order, war and ecological disaster. Formulating complex chronologies of end-time events fulfils a desire to find a framework to make sense of historical events. I aim to show that the millennium of Revelation is in fact highly relevant to these concerns, although in a more profound way than is sometimes realized.

Why Do We Have Problems With This Text?

I have already mentioned that Revelation 20 features rarely in sermons and Bible studies in churches in this country. I believe that there are three key reasons for this.

First, Revelation as a whole is a practically closed book in many churches. Aside from series of sermons on the letters to the seven churches in chapters 2–3, and the occasional reference to the New Jerusalem of chapters 21–22, the text is hardly addressed. The great sequence of chapters 4–20, with its themes of the sovereignty and justice of God, the lordship of Christ, and the vindication of God's people, is neglected, partly because of its difficult imagery. The millennium suffers along with the rest of this central section of the book. I shall try to tackle this problem by placing the millennium firmly in the context of Revelation as a whole, to show how it illuminates key themes running through the entire book.

Second, there is reluctance to engage with Revelation 20 because of the detailed arguments which the millennium has aroused. Much of the discussion about this passage has involved the construction of complex-sounding schemes with technical names: premillennialism, postmillennialism, amillennialism, and so on. We shall look at these later on. But it is perfectly understandable that preachers are wary of being drawn into what appears to be a doctrinal quagmire of obscure detail. And the questions with which these schemes often seem to be primarily concerned, such as the nature and duration of the millennial kingdom, seem difficult to integrate with the wider message of the New Testament. I shall try to tackle this problem by bringing out the theological importance of the millennium, and showing that it does indeed relate to the great overarching themes of the gospel.

Third, throughout the history of the church, focus on the millennium has often been associated with extreme movements. Some groups have acted violently in the belief they were preparing for the onset of the millennium.[4] Others have suffered lasting trauma through predicting a date for the return of Christ, only to be bitterly disappointed by his non-appearance.[5] This exotic and disturbing inheritance has understandably led to great caution in the use of the text.

I shall attempt to allay these concerns by showing that the millennium might effectively be acommodated within a 'mainstream' Christian understanding.

---

4   The classic case is the anabaptist movement in Münster in 1533-5, the most notorious leader of which was John of Leyden. For an account of this episode, see Norman Cohn, *The Pursuit of the Millennium* (London: Paladin, 1970) pp 252-80.
5   See, for example, the case of the Millerites in 1840s America, described in Stephen O'Leary, *Arguing the Apocalypse* (New York & Oxford: OUP, 1994) chs 4-5.

2
Reading the Book of Revelation

Ways of Approaching the Text

Centuries of reflection on the book of Revelation have produced a bewildering array of ways of interpreting it. Some commentators have argued that the text relates entirely to events in the first century, providing a symbolic interpretation of the tribulations of the church at the time the book was written. This line of interpretation is fine as far as it goes. But the book's message cannot be limited to the first century. It is relevant to the world now and it makes important claims about the ultimate future.

Others have seen in the text a symbolic account of the whole of human history. Again, there is something to be said for this. As Scripture, Revelation is relevant at all times and in all places. The problem with this kind of interpretation is that those following it have tended to assume that the historical process culminates in their own day. This means that interpretation becomes dominated by the interpreter's own particular agenda (for example, most of the reformers understood the beast of Revelation to represent the papacy) and that one such interpretation is rapidly succeeded by another as time rolls on. Another problem with this method is that it often fails to show what relevance the book would have had for its first readers.

A third approach is to see Revelation as a set of predictive prophecies relating entirely to the end-times. The assumption behind this approach is often that the end-times are beginning in the interpreter's own day, and that features of the text can be taken to stand for contemporary people, places or events. A recent example of this method is the claim that Rev 8.11, speaking of a star named Wormwood falling to earth, is a prediction of the Chernobyl disaster, on the grounds that Chernobyl is Russian for wormwood.

Fourth, some interpreters have sought to detect timeless principles in the text about the way in which God deals with humanity. The events in the text are held to represent these themes symbolically. This approach has much to commend it, in enabling the interpreter to draw out key theological themes. The danger is that the text becomes a kind of free-floating set of abstract principles, divorced from its historical setting, and without a real sense of expectation of future fulfilment.

Some Key Principles

In fact, a successful interpretation of the text probably needs to draw to a greater or lesser extent on all of the above approaches. The approach I have taken in this booklet is therefore based on four key principles.

1. An interpretation must take account of the original circumstances in which the text arose, as far as possible.

Our knowledge of the background to the writing of Revelation is sketchy. The authorship and date of the text are disputed, although most modern commentators argue that it was written in Asia Minor by a church leader named John (probably not the apostle), about 96AD. It is clear that at least some of the Christian communities to whom John wrote were suffering oppression.[6] But the evidence for a systematic persecution of Christians in that part of the Roman empire at that time is thin. Many modern commentators have suggested that John's purpose in writing was not to sustain a church already undergoing persecution. Instead, his purpose was to warn Christians against compromise with surrounding pagan culture.[7] Standing out in this way would be likely to provoke persecution, but John assures his readers that God will triumph over evil and vindicate his people.

2. John's main aim in writing Revelation was to reveal truth about the present situation of his readers.

This follows on from the first principle. An interpretation which sees the text simply as a prediction of events perhaps hundreds of years in the future is unlikely to be adequate. John certainly writes about the future, but he does so in order to enable his readers to understand more clearly their own context, and their place in the overall purposes of God. As Richard Bauckham puts it, '[John] is given a glimpse behind the scenes of history so that he can see what is really going on in the events of his time and place. He is also transported in vision into the final future of the world, so that he can see the present from the perspective of what its final outcome must be, in God's ultimate purpose for human history.'[8]

3. Revelation deals with the past, present and future of the world.

Although John's purpose is to speak to the present situation of his readers, it would be a great mistake to reduce the relevance of the text to some kind of timeless, ever-present set of principles. God's sovereignty and justice are as yet largely hidden in the world of John's readers and in our world also but there will come a point when they are manifest to all. Some of John's readers were suffering persecution, and more would come to suffer in the days ahead, just as many Christians do still, but there will come a point when they are vindicated, and their suffering ceases.[9]

---

6 See for example 2.9, 2.13.

7 A good introductory account of the possible social situation of Revelation is in John Sweet's commentary (London: SCM, 1979) pp 27-35. For a more detailed study, see Leonard Thompson, *The Book of Revelation: Apocalypse and Empire* (New York: OUP, 1990).

8 *The Theology of the Book of Revelation* (Cambridge University Press, 1993) p 7.

9 For an application of the message of Revelation to a modern situation of oppression, South

4. Revelation is written in apocalyptic language, which by its very nature is symbolic.

John drew on an established stock of apocalyptic imagery (beasts, horns, a dragon, celestial armies, and so on), which would have been familiar to his first readers. By and large, this language is not to be read as some kind of complex code, in which each symbol serves merely as a simple sign for something else in a one-for-one relationship. So the example I gave above, of equating Wormwood with Chernobyl is, I would argue, misguided. Rather, the language is *multivalent*—that is, it triggers off several, maybe many, different associations in the readers mind. For example, it is quite clear that John uses the symbol of Babylon, the great city, to refer primarily to Rome. Yet 'Babylon' would of course have triggered associations from the past history of Israel, as the oppressor which had taken the people into exile. And there is a sense in which the symbol of Babylon in Revelation can be confined to no particular city. In 18.24, it is said that in Babylon 'was found the blood…of all who have been slaughtered on earth,' something which was true of neither the historical Rome nor the historical Babylon. The symbol presses on beyond any particular identification, to represent human society wherever it is in revolt against God.

Pulling these principles together, I would suggest that it is a mistake to look for neat chronological patterns in the text. John is not giving his readers a calendar of history. But he *is* placing their present experience in an ultimate perspective which takes in the past, present and future. He writes about what we might call the penultimate future, when God's people are oppressed by God's enemies, and God executes his judgment upon those enemies. John also writes about the ultimate future of everlasting peace and security in the presence of God in the New Jerusalem. The key to interpreting the way time works in Revelation is to see how John's categories of the past, present, penultimate future and ultimate future relate to each other, rather than to try to detect a detailed chronology of events. And the millennium plays an important bridging role between the present and the ultimate future. It depicts the manifest establishment of God's rule in a way which transcends our present experience, and is a clear anticipation of the ultimate future. But it is not yet the ultimate future, since it is set on the old earth, and is in turn transcended by the creation of the new heaven and new earth and the descent of the New Jerusalem.[10]

Africa under apartheid, see Allan Boesak, *Comfort and Protest* (Edinburgh: St Andrew Press, 1987).

10 See my discussion in chapter 5 of the theme of God's commitment to this earth.

3

Four Interpretations of the Text

My purpose in this section is not to give a detailed account of the different ways of approaching the text, nor the history of how they arose. Such information is relatively readily available elsewhere, and I have given some suggested reading in the bibliography. What follows is a brief description of each of the four main ways in which the text has been handled in the history of the church.

Classical Premillennialism[11]

Premillennialism was the most widely-held view in the earliest church. Papias, Justin, Irenaeus and Tertullian were all premillennialists. According to this view, Revelation 19–20 should be read as a single sequence, so that the parousia will happen first, then Satan will be bound, and the millennium will follow. The millennium will be a literal kingdom, located on earth, lasting for a thousand years.[12] The resurrection mentioned in 20.4 ('the first resurrection') is therefore a physical resurrection on earth.

One advantage of this view is that it takes the text of Revelation 19–20 in what seems on the surface to be its natural order. It does not require that 20.1 be seen as 'stepping back' behind the time of the parousia, but simply takes the whole passage as one sequence. This interpretation also has the advantage of grounding God's eschatological act firmly in an earthly context, underlining his commitment to the world and its future. Another strength is that this is the view held by the earliest church.

Classical premillennialism suffers from several disadvantages, however. It builds a great deal on one biblical reference. There is no unambiguous support for a premillennial position anywhere else in Scripture.[13] Critics of this position question why there should be a need for an interim kingdom,

---

11 I have followed David Pawson in labelling the premillennialism which was characteristic of the early church 'classical' to distinguish it from most modern premillennialism, which is dispensationalist (see below). Classical premillennialism still has its supporters today. See the essay by George Ladd in the volume edited by Clouse, and Pawson's recent book, *When Jesus Comes*, both listed in the bibliography.

12 Some classical premillennialists, such as Pawson (*When Jesus Comes*, pp 216-7) take the reference to a thousand years literally. Others take it symbolically, to refer to a period of unspecified duration; see George Ladd, *A Commentary on the Revelation of John* (Grand Rapids: Eerdmans, 1972) p 262.

13 Some have seen a possible reference to the millennium in 1 Cor 15.23-4, which it is possible to interpret as positing a delay between the parousia and the final eschatological consummation. However, this is probably an unwarranted conclusion to draw from the text. For a discussion of the exegetical issues, see Gordon Fee, *The First Epistle to the Corinthians* (Grand Rapids: Eerdmans, 1987) pp 751-4.

following the return of Christ, which continues to fall short of the eternal perfection of the ultimate future described in the vision of the New Jerusalem. Another potential difficulty with this position is that it can degenerate into an excessively materialistic vision of the future. This was certainly one of the reasons why premillennialism fell out of favour by the time of Augustine.[14]

Amillennialism

The amillennialist interpretation developed by Augustine in Book XX of his great work, *The City of God*, has been of immense influence ever since. Contrary to what the term may suggest, amillennialism in this sense does not mean the lack of belief in any millennium at all. Rather, it rejects the idea of a millennium taking place in a specific future period of time.

Amillennialism does not take Revelation 19–20 to run in a single sequence, but understands the passage on the millennium to be a step back in time to a point before the parousia of chapter 19. In fact, 20.1 is seen as stepping right back to the earthly life of Jesus. The binding of Satan is linked to statements in the gospel narratives, such as the parable of the binding of the strong man (Mt 12.29, Mk 3.27, Lk 11.21–2). The exorcisms of Jesus' ministry were illustrations of the fact that Satan had already been bound. On this view, the millennium is not a specific future period of exactly a thousand years, but is rather a symbolic representation of the whole of the period between the earthly life of Jesus and the parousia. The resurrection of 20.4 is seen as a spiritual resurrection referring to those who have died for their faith in Christ and are even now reigning with him in heaven, or perhaps referring to Christians more generally, who have been spiritually regenerated.[15]

This interpretation has several important advantages compared with classical premillennialism. By treating the millennium in a symbolic way, not limiting it to a literal, earthly kingdom, this approach perhaps does more justice to the symbolic nature of apocalyptic language. It is easier to integrate with the message of the New Testament as a whole, partly because of the connection it makes with the gospel tradition, and partly because the elimination of the idea of an interim kingdom after the parousia appears more consistent with the eschatological picture offered elsewhere in the New Testament. And making the millennium represent the present church age

---

14 For example, Eusebius (c260—340AD), wrote that the heretic Cerinthus viewed the millennial kingdom as a time of 'the gratification of appetite and lust; that is ...eating, drinking, and marrying,' and that the Egyptian bishop Nepos supposed that there would be a certain millennium of sensual luxury on this earth (*Ecclesiastical History* 3.38, 7.24).

15 A brief account of the passage from an amillennialist perspective is in Michael Wilcock's volume in the Bible Speaks Today series, *The Message of Revelation* (Leicester & Downers Grove: IVP, 1975) pp 187-91.

makes it appear more immediately relevant to Christians now.

However, like classical premillennialism, it suffers from various disadvantages. It relies upon the assumption that 20.1 represents a step back from the parousia to an earlier point. Critics of amillennialism argue that a cyclical pattern is being forced onto the text at this point in order to buttress a preconceived theological position. Certainly, a straightforward reading of the text would suggest that, for John, the millennium is a symbol relating to the future, not the present. In addition, some amillennialists require that *ezesan* ('came to life') be translated in two completely different ways in the space of two verses, the first time to reflect the spiritual resurrection of the martyrs to rule with Christ in heaven, and the second time to represent the physical resurrection of the rest of the dead at the last judgment. Critics argue that this is implausible.

Postmillennialism

Like amillennialism, postmillennialism sees Revelation 20.1 as stepping back to a point in time before the parousia. However, unlike amillennialism, it locates that point, not at the time of the incarnation, but at some point in the subsequent history of the world. The millennium is therefore a particular period within the history of the present age, at the end of which Christ will return. This period opens with the binding of Satan, which then allows a new age to dawn and flourish. Some postmillennialists have seen this in spiritual terms, arguing that signs of the millennium include such things as the spread of the gospel to all parts of the globe. Others have seen the millennium more in terms of social and political progress. Postmillennialism first became popular as a result of the teachings of Joachim of Fiore in the twelfth century, who predicted the dawning of a new age of the Spirit. Later, its influence spread alongside optimistic theories of historical progress in the eighteenth and nineteenth centuries. The terrible experiences of this century have largely undermined confidence in postmillennialism, and today it is very much a minority position.[16]

The disadvantages I noted above in respect of amillennialism also apply to postmillennialism. It is also open to the criticism that whereas its advocates have often argued that the new millennial age has already dawned, it is difficult to see evidence for this in the real world.

Dispensational Premillennialism

Partly in response to the loss of confidence in postmillennialism, there has been a strong resurgence in premillennialism since the last century. Today

---

16 See the essay by Boettner in the volume edited by Clouse (in the bibliography) for a rare recent defence of postmillennialism. It is not very convincing!

this usually takes the form of dispensational premillennialism, which is widely popular in North America and the growing churches of the developing world. Like classical premillennialism, dispensational premillennialism assumes that the millennium is a literal earthly kingdom which will follow the parousia. But there are key differences from the classical position.

Dispensationalism is associated in particular with the nineteenth century figure of J N Darby, one of the founders of the Brethren movement, and with the *Scofield Reference Bible*, first published in 1909, and still widely used today. The main feature of dispensationalism is a belief that God's relationship with humanity has taken the form of different dispensations through history, in which God has taken a distinct initiative requiring a response from humanity. For our purposes, there are two key points. First, the system envisages two different dispensations, one applying to Israel, the other to the church. Second, dispensationalism relies on a heavily literalistic method of biblical interpretation. The combination of these two factors leads dispensationalists to argue that the Old Testament promises of the glorious restoration of an earthly Israel should be taken literally. The promises have clearly not yet been fulfilled literally, and dispensationalists look to the millennium for their fulfilment.[17] Precise details of dispensationalist schemes vary, but all envisage a key role for the Jews in the millennium. Alongside this belief is the distinctive doctrine of the rapture, according to which believers will be secretly removed from earth to heaven.[18] This will be followed by a period of great tribulation, at the end of which Christ will return and the millennial kingdom will be established, centred on Jerusalem.

The disadvantages I noted earlier in respect of classical premillennialism also apply to dispensational premillennialism. Its critics have also questioned its highly literalistic hermeneutic and its assumption that we should look for a literal future fulfilment of Old Testament prophecy, rather than, for example, seeing its fulfilment in Christ. And it is not clear why the promises of restoration in, for example Isaiah 11, should be seen as relating to an interim kingdom, rather than as symbolic references to the ultimate eschatological future.

---

17 A feature of some contemporary premillennial schemes is their search for signs of the approaching end in contemporary affairs. This often involves identifying nations or individuals with particular symbols drawn from biblical eschatology. A particularly persistent example of this is the identification of contemporary Russia (or, before 1991, the Soviet Union) with *Meshech* in Ezekiel 38.2 (*Meshech* sounds like Moscow). Another is the identification of the European Union with the ten toes of the statue in Daniel 2. The expansion of the EU to include more than ten members has done little to quell this particular theory. This kind of speculation is in fact rather in tension with strict dispensationalism, which assumes that the rapture of believers, before the great tribulation, will be unexpected, and therefore not preceded by signs.

18 The imagery associated with the rapture is drawn especially from 1 Thess 4.13-18. The text often used to apply this imagery to a secret rapture before the great tribulation is Revelation 3.10 ('...I will keep you from the hour of trial...').

Problems With These Approaches

Those on all sides of the debate should recognize that their fellow-Christians might quite legitimately hold different views from themselves on this subject. All four of the views I have described have their attractions and their distinguished supporters. At the same time, none of the four positions is without its problems. Each, as we have seen, throws up particular difficulties, both with regard to the text, and more generally. My personal view is that the amillennial position is the most convincing of the four. But even that position, in its widely-understood, Augustinian form, suffers from the fundamental weakness that it effectively de-eschatologizes what appears to be a firmly eschatological text. The sense of future expectation which runs through the passage, as in the rest of Revelation, is seriously diminished.

However, as I suggested at the end of the previous section, this whole debate may be focusing on the wrong issues. A great deal of effort is expended on questions of 'when?' and 'where?' but not nearly enough on 'why?' The debate has the effect of cramping the discussion of the *theological* importance of the text.[19] Second, little attempt is made to see how the message of the millennium related to the themes of the rest of Revelation, let alone the themes of the gospel as a whole. Third, it becomes very difficult to make use of the text in teaching and preaching. People give up on it as being what George Caird described as 'the paradise of cranks and fanatics on the one hand and literalists on the other.'[20]

I am not suggesting that debates of the kind we have seen between the four positions outlined above are invalid, or that we cannot learn from the views I have described. But in the rest of the booklet, I suggest that there are other ways of looking at the text which are illuminating and which help to show more clearly its relevance for Christian faith.

---

19 It is surprising that many interpreters who are content to take, for example, the sequences of seals, trumpets and bowls in a symbolic way, apparently get waylaid by a more literalistic agenda when they reach Revelation 20, and ask the sort of 'when' and 'where' questions they would not begin to pose in relation to other parts of the book.

20 *The Revelation of St John the Divine* (London: A&C Black, 1984 [2nd ed]) p 249.

4
The Origin of the Symbol of the Millennium

I have already mentioned that one of the difficulties with Revelation 20 is that the idea of the millennium does not occur explicitly anywhere else in Scripture. However, the idea did not just appear from nowhere.

Although the millennium cannot be found in the Old Testament, prophecies of the earthly restoration of Israel certainly can. For our purposes, perhaps the most significant of these prophecies is at the end of the book of Ezekiel. In chapter 37, the well-known vision of the valley of dry bones is followed by an assurance from God that Israel will be gathered together from among the nations. The people will obey God's law unequivocally and prosper in a peaceful kingdom, in the promised land, ruled over by a Davidic messiah.[21] In Ezekiel, this is followed by an attack by a huge enemy army— led by Gog, of the land of Magog—which is defeated by God (38.1–39.22). Then, in chapters 40ff, comes Ezekiel's great vision of the restored temple.

The idea of an interim kingdom before the last judgment is found most clearly, apart from in Revelation itself, in two Jewish apocalypses, 4 Ezra and 2 Baruch, which most scholars date to around the same time as Revelation, near the end of the first century AD. In 4 Ezra 7.26–44 there is a prophecy of a messianic kingdom which will last for four hundred years, at the end of which the messiah and all of humanity will die. Then comes the last judgment, with eternal rest for the righteous and torment for the wicked. In 2 Baruch 29, it is said that the coming of the messiah will be accompanied by a time of great plenty, in which the earth will yield its fruits ten-thousand-fold. 'On one vine will be a thousand branches, and one branch will produce a thousand clusters, and one cluster will produce a thousand grapes, and one grape will produce a cor [that is, about forty litres] of wine.' The following chapter then refers to the last judgment.

It seems that in both 4 Ezra and 2 Baruch we can see a combination of two different traditions of hope for the future. The first, drawn from the Hebrew prophetic tradition, looked forward to an earthly restoration of Israel. However, with the fall of the Israelite monarchies and the exile, a second tradition developed. Confidence in a restoration within history was eroded, and in the genre of apocalyptic literature which flourished in post-exilic times hope was increasingly focused on the idea of salvation beyond this age, to be brought in by a radical inbreaking initiative of God. In 4 Ezra and 2 Baruch, the interim messianic kingdom appears to be the result of combining these

---

21 Similar prophecies can be found in, for example, Isaiah 11 and Jeremiah 31.

two ideas, so that there is in effect a composite hope, first for a renewal of an earthly Israel, and then for God's ultimate saving act, which will transcend earthly existence.

There are clear parallels between the millennium in Revelation and these passages in Jewish apocalyptic of the same period. There are also important differences. In 4 Ezra and 2 Baruch, the interim kingdom has a purely earthly character. There is no suggestion that people will come back to life to participate in it. And Revelation 20 is the only passage to set the duration of the interim kingdom at a thousand years. Many commentators trace this period of time back to the ancient idea that the history of the world corresponds to a great 'week,' each day of which lasts a thousand years (compare Psalm 90.4).

Nonetheless, we have established that, at the time John was writing, there were other ideas around which bore a strong similarity to the millennium of Revelation 20. While that still does not explain what the purpose of the millennium might be in the context of Revelation (we shall come to that in the next section), it does give us important background. In particular, we have seen that the pattern of an interim kingdom followed by the last judgment followed by the ultimate eschatological future may represent the combination of two ideas, one emphasizing the outworking of God's purposes *within* history, the other emphasizing God's plan to transform this age into a completely new one.

5
Making the Millennium Relevant

The aim of this section is to map out an alternative (or perhaps complementary) approach to the text which I believe enables its theological significance to be more readily grasped, and enables it to be used more easily in teaching and preaching. The approach I am taking is based on the four key principles I set out at the end of chapter 2 as guidelines for interpreting the book of Revelation: that interpretation should take account of the original circumstances in which the text arose; that John's primary aim is to reveal truth about the present situation of his readers; that he does this by setting their situation in an overall framework of the past, present and future purposes of God; and that we must do justice to the symbolic nature of apocalyptic language. I went on to suggest that it is misguided to seek precise chronologies of history in Revelation, and that a more promising approach is to look at the way John interrelates different temporal *categories*, especially those of the present, the penultimate future, and the ultimate future.

The approach I am suggesting assumes that the millennium is set on earth, in the future, in John's scheme. So, like the premillennialist, I take chs 19–20 of Revelation to flow together in a single sequence. I believe this is a more straightforward reading of the text. But I am also concerned to do justice to the symbolic nature of apocalyptic language. So, unlike the premillennialist, I do not assume that we should look for a literal fulfilment of this passage in an interim kingdom. Like many other passages in Revelation, 20.1–6 is symbolic. This does *not* mean it is fiction. It conveys key truths about God's relations with the world and with his people. Nor does it mean reducing the text to a set of timeless abstractions. I want to affirm strongly the Christian expectation that Christ will return and that God will act to transform this world and to vindicate his people—and that this will actually happen in the future. My argument is that the symbol of the millennium tells us important truths about this event, rather than itself expressing literally what will happen.

I have set out below four key themes which come together in the symbol of the millennium. These themes run right through Revelation, so that this approach helps to integrate 20.1–6 more readily with the rest of the text than other approaches often do. These themes are also great themes of the New Testament as a whole, so this approach enables the symbol of the millennium to be integrated more effectively into an overall understanding of the New Testament. I hope this will give readers more confidence in preaching and teaching on the millennium in its own right, as well as referring to the millennium to support teaching centred on other passages of Scripture.

The Triumph of God

The eschatological triumph of God is one of the central themes of Revelation. One of the key messages John seeks to convey to his readers in first century Asia Minor, as they face the possibility of persecution, is that despite all appearances to the contrary, God really is sovereign over the universe. By revealing the certainty of the ultimate victory of God over his enemies (Satan, death, the beast and the great whore), John enables his readers to see their current situation in its true overall context. The letters to the seven churches in chapters 2 and 3 describe a setting in which Christians are often under pressure to conform to the surrounding pagan culture, and sometimes suffering severely. Yet chapter 4 describes the glorious reality of God's sovereignty in heaven. There is therefore an apparent contradiction. Much of the remainder of the text is a grand panoramic description, in symbolic terms, of the way in which the sovereignty of God becomes a manifest reality on the earthly plane, and not only in heaven, so that the contradiction is resolved. The process culminates with the descent from heaven to earth of the New Jerusalem in chapter 21.

The millennium is a critical stage in this process. It is the first point in the text at which the sovereignty of God is openly manifest on earth. The sequences of judgment on the enemies of God (interspersed with assurances of salvation for his people) which have formed the substance of 6.1–19.11 take place in a framework in which divine action is initiated in heaven, with earthly effect. This is graphically illustrated, for example, by the pouring out of the seven bowls of wrath onto the earth in chapter 16. At 19.11, however, this pattern is dramatically altered as the heavens open and Christ returns to earth. Now that the long process of judgment (which has included opportunities for repentance: 9.20–1, 16.8–11) is over, the time has come for the sovereignty of God to be manifest on earth itself. The enemies of God have been defeated. The beast and the false prophet have been consigned to the lake of fire (19.20) and Satan is bound. The justice of God can be dispensed openly by his servants (20.4).

The confident expectation of the ultimate triumph of God over the powers of evil is a message the contemporary church needs to hear no less than did John's readers. Seeing the millennium in this light suggests immediate linkages to other New Testament passages.

One obvious example is 1 Corinthians 15. Paul draws out the consequences of God's victory over death in the raising of Christ. As Beker puts it, 'The death of Christ shatters the alliance of the apocalyptic powers and signals the imminent overthrow of death, the last enemy.'[22] Just as Paul can give thanks for the triumph of God over the powers of sin and death (1 Cor 15.57),

---

22 J C Beker, *The Triumph of God* (Minneapolis: Fortress, 1990) p 81.

so the millennium affirms the victory of God and the re-establishment of his just rule over the world.[23]

The triumph of God is indicated dramatically by the binding of Satan in 20.2. This enables the peace and justice of the millennial kingdom to flourish, a point underlined by the brief chaos which ensues on Satan's temporary release in 20.7.[24] I mentioned earlier that the Augustinian amillennialist position assumes that the binding of Satan implies that chapter 20 'steps back' to the time of Jesus' earthly ministry. There are certainly connections between events in Jesus' ministry and Revelation 20.2, which again help to link the millennium to a wider understanding of the New Testament. A particularly striking case comes in the story of the Gerasene demoniac in Mark 5.[25] Jesus has mentioned the binding of Satan in Mk 3.27, and this is fulfilled in Mk 5.1ff, with the casting out of Legion into the herd of pigs. As Rowland points out, the parallel account in Luke describes the demons as begging not to be dispatched into the abyss—the same word as in Revelation 20.3. However, as I have argued, the Augustinian amillennialist reading of the text is unconvincing in its assumption that 20.1ff is a step back to the ministry of Jesus. The connection between these gospel accounts and the eschatological expectation of the binding of Satan may therefore be more plausibly seen as one of anticipation. As Rowland argues, 'The integration of the individual in the gospel story [that is, the Gerasene demoniac] is a proleptic glimpse of that harmony which will come in the millennium, when fragmented lives have been restored and the disorder which masquerades as peace has been overcome.'[26]

The Lordship of Christ

Richard Bauckham has rightly argued that 'Revelation has the most developed trinitarian theology in the New Testament, with the possible exception of the Gospel of John.'[27] The great process of the establishment of the sovereignty of God on earth, to which I referred in the previous paragraph, is in fact triggered in the text by the appearance of Christ. It is the Lamb who, in 5.5, is deemed the only one in heaven or earth worthy to open the

---

23 See also Romans 6.7-10; 8.31-9; Col 2.15.

24 Satan is released in 20.7, at the end of the thousand years, and leads a final rebellion against God and his elect, although the episode simply results in Satan's destruction. Explanations of this strange passage vary greatly. One of the more convincing ones is that the passage serves to illustrate that until the complete cosmic transformation of chapters 21-2, the earth will remain prone to disobedience, no matter how apparently peaceful and secure it is. This argument is advanced by, for example, G R Beasley-Murray, *The Book of Revelation* (London: Marshall, Morgan and Scott, 1978) pp 291-2.

25 See the excellent brief discussion in Christopher Rowland, *Revelation* (London: Epworth, 1993) pp 149-50.

26 Rowland, *Revelation*, p 150.

27 *The Theology of the Book of Revelation*, p 164.

sealed scroll and thus begin the first series of judgments. It is the Lamb around whom the community of the saints forms, as they follow the path of sacrifice which he has laid out for them (7.13–17; 12.11; 14.1–5; 19.6–9). And the Lamb becomes so closely identified with God that it is difficult to distinguish them (21.22; 22.1). The millennium is, again, a critical point in the development of this theme. Those who have died for the sake of Christ now rule with him (20.4, 6).

At many points in Revelation, ironic contrasts are made between the Lamb and the beast. The beast has been wounded (13.3), as has the Lamb (5.6). The beast has two horns like a lamb (13.11). The beast has a mysterious name (13.18), as does the Lamb (2.17, 3.12). In a sense, the beast is partly a parody of the Lamb. But at the millennium, this pretence is blown apart totally. The beast, a source of deception and cruel disorder, is in the lake of fire, while Christ, the Lamb, establishes a just order, in which those whom the beast thought he had destroyed come back to life.

Tracing the theme of the lordship of Christ through Revelation, and recognizing the importance of the millennial kingdom in this context, suggests connections with other key New Testament passages. For example, Phil 2.5–11 sets out the same pattern of self-abasement, sacrifice and exaltation. Christ's obedience unto death (Phil 2.6–8; cf Rev 5.6,9,12) is followed by his glorious triumph (Phil 2.9–11; cf Rev 5.9ff).[28] Interestingly, in both passages, the inhabitants of heaven, the earth, and under the earth, are said to glorify Christ (Phil 2.10; cf Rev 5.13).[29]

God's Vindication of his People

I have mentioned at several points so far the importance of doing justice to the original context in which the text arose. The evidence for any kind of systematic persecution of Christians at this date is thin. But John is clearly urging his readers against accommodation with the surrounding pagan society, where to do so would compromise their faith. There had been at least one recent martyrdom in the churches to whom he wrote (2.13). The description of the cry of the martyrs under the altar at 6.9–11 emphasizes that John expected more to follow. Several passages in Revelation describe the expectation of an imminent period of severe tribulation for the church as a whole (7.13–18; 11.3–13;12.17;13.7,15).

Revelation reveals dimensions of reality which were otherwise hidden. For John's readers this meant, crucially, that the apparent defeat and failure of martyrdom would, in an ultimate perspective, turn out to have been a glorious victory. The beast might enjoy an apparent victory lasting for three

---

28 See also Heb 2.9.
29 The Greek expressions are not identical, but they convey the same thought.

and a half years (13.5), but the resurrected martyrs would rule for much longer, a thousand years, and would then continue to live and reign with God in the New Jerusalem.[30] The significance of the symbol of the millennium in this regard is that the martyrs are vindicated by God on earth, the place in which they originally suffered, thus emphasizing the complete defeat of the forces that oppressed them. As Jürgen Moltmann comments, 'It would be a confutation of their martyrdom if God were not to show his power at the very point where, for him and with him, they suffered in his helplessness, and if God were not to assert his rights in the very situation in which they were executed.'[31]

So the millennium represents the vindication of the people of God. As with the other two themes I have dealt with above, this enables connections to be made with other parts of Scripture. There is a particularly illuminating set of connections with the Old Testament tradition of exodus and liberation. A well-known Old Testament tradition of anticipates the eschatological exodus of the people of God (Isaiah 11.11–12.6; 43.14–21; 51.10–11). Revelation picks up this theme clearly in the reference to Balaam as a source of false teaching (2.14), the links between the death of Christ and the Passover lamb (5.6, 9–10), the Song of Moses (15.2–4), and the parallels between the bowls judgments of chapter 16 and the plagues of Exodus 7–12. The theme of the intervention of God to free his people from oppression has inspired the use of Revelation in the context of liberation theology, a notable recent example being Allan Boesak's book, *Comfort and Protest*.[32]

God's Commitment to Transform this Earth

In Revelation, John seeks to expand the horizons of his readers' understanding by revealing ultimate dimensions of reality, within which to locate their present experience. One aspect of this is the anticipation of the ultimate consummation of God's plan for the world. This plan culminates in the descent of the New Jerusalem. The language is symbolic, and it would be wrong to try to pin it down too precisely. But it seems clear that the eschaton is envisaged not merely as a sudden inbreaking of an utterly new framework of reality, as a means of escape from the world. The New Jerusalem comes

---

30 See the very helpful discussion in Bauckham, *The Theology of the Book of Revelation*, pp 106-8. Bauckham understands the millennium to vindicate the martyrs. There is in fact exegetical disagreement over whether those ruling with Christ in 20.4 and 6 should be taken to include only those who have been martyred for Christ, or the whole of the church. The dispute turns on whether there is only one group in view (those who had been beheaded for their testimony), or whether there is an addition a second group, who had not necessarily been beheaded, but who had still refused to worship the beast. Commentators such as Caird, Beasley-Murray, Giblin and Bauckham assume only martyrs are meant. Others (eg Swete, Ladd, Roloff and Sweet) assume there are two groups. The Greek can be translated in either sense.

31 *The Coming of God* (London: SCM, 1996) p 152.

32 See note 9 above.

from heaven, that is true, but it descends to earth, amid God's creation of a new heaven and a new earth. So God's eschatological act includes the transformation of this earth, not its obliteration.

I have suggested that the millennium should be understood as a symbol which conveys truth about the nature of the eschatological future. Since it is set on earth, it has a key role in emphasizing the hope for the transformation of this world.[33] As Roloff comments:

[the millennium is] a reference to an important aspect of New Testament eschatology that Christianity repeatedly suppressed to its and the world's detriment. Because God is Creator and Lord of history, his salvation also addresses this world and its history. God creates his new world not because he would be powerless to secure a place for himself and those who belong to him in the old one, but rather because he wills and has promised something even greater. The new creation is not denial and abandonment of the old, but rather the surpassing of it.[34]

Caird expresses this point particularly well: 'There must come a time on earth when it is true to say: "the sovereignty of the world has passed to our God and to his Christ." Unless the world is moving to such a goal, Christ has won only a Pyrrhic victory which, whatever the theologians may claim, leaves the powers of evil in possession.'[35] This is in tune with the central theme in Revelation as a whole of the establishment of the manifest rule of God on the earthly plane.

The presence of the millennium in Revelation 20 therefore serves to guard against an overemphasis on discontinuity in eschatology. It marks a new stage in God's eschatological plan, yet it is set in the context of this earth (the new heaven and earth do not appear until 21.1). As such, it constitutes an important bridge between this age and the ultimate future, emphasizing that God's transformation of the cosmos involves an element of continuity as well as discontinuity.

This provides an important link to other eschatological accounts in the New Testament. For example, the same emphasis on both continuity and discontinuity is present in Paul's treatment of personal eschatology in 1 Cor 15. Paul argues that the believer's body will be transformed in resurrection, but that there will be an element of continuity also. This is made clear in

---

3 3 See my comments in section 5 about the origins of the idea of the interim messianic kingdom as a combination of hope in God's salvation both within history and from beyond history.
3 4 Roloff, *Revelation* (Minneapolis: Fortress, 1993) p 226. See also the helpful discussion in Christopher Rowland, *Revelation* (London: Epworth, 1993) pp 147-52. Rowland argues that the millennium represents the fulfilment of the petition in the Lord's Prayer that 'thy will be done on earth as it is in heaven' (p 147).
3 5 Caird, *Revelation*, p 254.

Paul's discussion of the nature of the resurrection body in 1 Cor 15.35–41. He uses the picture of a seed and a plant as an analogy of the relationship between the believer's earthly body and the believer's resurrection body. There is an organic connection between a seed and the plant which grows from it, but at the same time the plant is a transformation of the seed. It is the same with the resurrection body, says Paul. Illuminating comparisons can be made with the gospel accounts of Jesus' resurrection appearances, in which he is recognized as the same Jesus, but also as transformed, and therefore not identical to the way he was before. Those he meets sometimes take time to recognize him, but are then sure of his identity (see especially the Emmaus road story in Luke 24.13–35 and Jesus' conversation with Mary Magdalene in John 20.11–18). This combination of continuity and discontinuity in the area of personal eschatology reinforces God's faithfulness both in his commitment to us as humans and in his commitment to transform us.

The message of Revelation, with its juxtaposition of the millennium and the creation of the new heaven and new earth, is that the same combination applies on the cosmic plane as well as on the personal plane. God is committed to this world and to its transformation. We need to be aware of this cosmic dimension of God's saving power as a counterbalance to an over-individualistic view. Christian social and political action should be informed by the continuity/discontinuity model. The church is not called merely to witness to continuity by blending in with its surroundings, nor is it called to practise discontinuity by cutting itself off from the world. In being in the world but not of the world, the church witnesses to God's transformative power, and to this eschatological balance between continuity and discontinuity.

6
Conclusion

In this booklet, I have argued that the millennium of Revelation 20 is a rich and powerful symbol with important implications for our understanding of God's relationship with the world. I have also suggested that the long-established debates between the various traditional approaches to the text (premillennialism, postmillennialism, amillennialism) tend sometimes to obscure the theological significance of the passage. The approach I have adopted is to see the millennium neither as the prediction of a literal future state, nor as a timeless abstraction. Rather, I have interpreted it as a symbol which conveys key truths about God's plan to execute his justice and renew the world. The symbol is situated in the future, but has profound implications for how we live now. In chapter 5, I have therefore sought to illustrate how the millennium can be effectively related to central themes of the book of Revelation and of Scripture more widely: the triumph of God, the lordship of Christ, God's vindication of his people, and God's commitment to transform the earth.

However, these great themes of Christian eschatology, to which the millennium of Revelation 20 gives particular focus, are of course relevant not only to debates within the church. At the beginning of this booklet, I mentioned that the phenomenon of end-time expectation goes far beyond the Christian churches. It has manifested itself in all kinds of forms, from certain New Age circles to the Branch Davidians. I also suggested that underlying this phenomenon there are real, deep-seated concerns, such as the desire to make sense of history, and to sustain a hope for the future amid war, famine, and ecological disaster. The biblical vision of the triumph of God, the lordship of Christ, God's vindication of his people, and his commitment to transform the earth, provides the church with compelling resources to speak prophetically and relevantly in this contemporary context. The symbol of the millennium helps us to affirm profound hope for the present and the future in the light of the ultimate power of God's love and justice. If this booklet has encouraged any of its readers to think further about how to engage with the truths of Christian eschatology—and Revelation 20 in particular—it will have achieved its purpose.

Bibliography

The following give brief, helpful comments on Revelation 20, from different viewpoints:

Richard Bauckham, *The Theology of the Book of Revelation* (CUP, 1993) pp 106–8. Sees the millennium as underlining the martyrs' victory.

George Caird, *Revelation* (London: A&C Black, 1984, 2nd edition) pp 248–58.

George Ladd, *A Commentary on the Revelation of John* (Grand Rapids: Eerdmans, 1972), pp 259–74. Written from a classical premillennialist perspective.

Robert Mounce, *The Book of Revelation* (Grand Rapids: Eerdmans, 1977) pp 351–60. Sets the passage in a premillennial scheme, without necessarily expecting a literal fulfilment.

Jürgen Roloff, *Revelation* (Minneapolis: Fortress, 1993) pp 222ff.

Christopher Rowland, *Revelation* (London: Epworth, 1993) pp 147ff. Emphasizes the political dimension of the millennium.

Michael Wilcock, *The Message of Revelation* (Leicester, Downers Grove : IVP, 1975) pp 187–94. Written from an amillennialist perspective.

Other treatments of the Millennium:

Paul Boyer, *When Time Shall Be No More: Prophecy Belief in Modern American Culture* (Cambridge MA: Harvard UP, 1992). Stimulating and perceptive account of contemporary American fundamentalist eschatology.

Robert G Clouse (ed), *The Meaning of the Millennium: Four Views* (Downers Grove: IVP, 1977). Covers classical premillennialism, dispensationalism, postmillennialism and amillennialism.

Norman Cohn, *The Pursuit of the Millennium* (London: Paladin, 1970). The classic account of millenarian movements in the Middle Ages.

J Webb Mealy, *After the Thousand Years: Resurrection and Judgment in Revelation 20* (Sheffield: JSOT Press, 1992). A very detailed recent examination of the text. Slightly idiosyncratic, but includes a helpful summary of different approaches to the text, and some stimulating theological insights.

Jürgen Moltmann, *The Coming of God: Christian Eschatology* (London: SCM, 1996). A stimulating account of eschatology from the perspective of systematic theology, with considerable discussion of the significance of the millennium.

Stephen O'Leary, *Arguing the Apocalypse: A Theory of Millennial Rhetoric* (New York: OUP, 1994). Interesting discussion of American millenarianism since the 19th century.

David Pawson, *When Jesus Returns* (London: Hodder, 1995). A recent defence of classical premillennialism.

Damian Thompson, *The End of Time* (London: Sinclair Stevenson, 1996). Deals with all kinds of pre-2000 speculation, both within the Christian church and outside it. Includes chapters on the Branch Davidians, New Age, and the Japanese Aum Shinrikyo cult.